MALAM, J.

John Cabot

Evans

Published by Evans Brothers Limited
2A Portman Mansions
Chiltern Street
London W1M 1LE

© Evans Brothers Limited 1997

First published 1997

Printed by Graficas Reunidas SA, Spain

ISBN 0 237 51764 7

British Library Cataloguing in Publication data.

Malam, John
 Tell me about John Cabot
 1. Cabot, John, ca. 1450-ca. 1499 – Juvenile literature
 2. Explorers – Biography – Juvenile literature 3. North
 America – Discovery and exploration – Juvenile literature
 I. Title II.John Cabot
 970' .01'092

John Cabot was an explorer. He lived such a long time ago that not much is known about him today. No one even knows what he really looked like.

We do know that he was born in about the year 1450, in a town in Italy. Some people think he came from a town called Genoa. Others say he was born near Naples. Both of these towns are by the sea.

This picture of John Cabot was painted in 1906. No one knows what he really looked like, so the artist has made it up.

When John was born his parents named him Giovanni Caboto. This was the name he was known by when he lived in Italy. Giovanni is the Italian name for John, and years later, when he lived in England, he changed his name to John Cabot.

This is a drawing of how Genoa looked in John's time.

John's last name tells us something interesting about his family. "Caboto" is the Italian word for "a sailor who sails near the coast". Because people were often named after the jobs they did, John might have come from a family of sailors.

This is a photograph of Genoa today. It is a busy port in Italy, just as it was in John's time.

When John was still a boy he went to live in another part of Italy. He moved to the city of Venice. It was a busy port with many boats and ships coming and going all the time.

Venice must have looked strange to John. It seemed to float on the sea. Its buildings were built on tiny islands of sand. The islands were surrounded by the sea. Instead of roads there were canals, and there were bridges everywhere.

A picture of Venice painted when John lived there.

Venice, in Italy, today. People use small boats to travel along the city's canals.

John's son, Sebastian, as an old man. He was a sailor and explorer, like his father.

John lived in Venice for many years.

He married a lady from Venice. Her name was Mattea. John and Mattea had three sons. They were Lewis, Sebastian and Sancio.

Alexandria, a trading city in North Africa.

John worked as a merchant. He sailed across the Mediterranean Sea to buy and sell goods.

John sailed in a little ship which had a crew of just a few men. He sailed from Venice to a city in North Africa called Alexandria. In Alexandria,

John bought spices such as pepper, nutmeg, cloves and cinnamon, brightly coloured silks and carpets, and medicines too. He took them back to Italy and sold them to rich people.

The goods came from Asia, a mysterious land far away to the east. Horses and camels carried them to Alexandria across mountains and deserts.

People in Europe wanted spices to make their food taste better.

Silks and spices were carried across deserts by camels, just as they are today.

11

Pilgrims in Mecca today. John went to Mecca disguised as a pilgrim.

Merchants in Alexandria told John about places they saw on their travels.

John wanted to see one of these exciting places for himself. He decided to go to Mecca, a Muslim

holy city. He went in disguise because he was not a Muslim himself.

John returned safely to Venice. He wanted to learn all he could about Asia, the mysterious land of silks and spices. He probably read a book called "A Description of the World" written by Marco Polo. He was an Italian traveller who had visited Asia long before John's time. Marco Polo's book was like a travel guide.

Marco Polo, a traveller from Venice who visited Asia. John Cabot probably read Marco Polo's book about Asia.

After some years, John and his family moved to Valencia, a city in Spain. John had work there.

A sailor called Christopher Columbus came to Valencia. He had important news. He said he had sailed to Asia by sailing around the globe to the west. It was a short-cut. No one had ever done this before.

Today we know that the land Columbus actually reached was the West Indies, a group of islands off the coast of America.

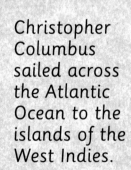

Christopher Columbus sailed across the Atlantic Ocean to the islands of the West Indies.

John wanted to sail to Asia too. He wanted to bring back spices and silks. But a long voyage across the Atlantic Ocean would be expensive. He asked the kings of Spain and Portugal for money. Both kings refused to help him.

The first ships to cross the Atlantic Ocean were very small. Sailors often had to sleep on the open deck.

John moved to England. He hoped someone there would pay for his voyage. The family settled in the city of Bristol. This was when John changed his name from Giovanni Caboto to John Cabot. It was easier for English people to say.

King Henry VII and the wealthy merchants of Bristol agreed to pay for John's voyage. They hoped he would bring valuable goods back from Asia which they could share.

A coin from King Henry VII's time. King Henry gave John money for his voyage.

King Henry VII of England

On John's first voyage across the Atlantic Ocean he ran out of food. He had to turn around and go back to England.

The following year, in May 1497, he tried again. With a crew of eighteen sailors, he sailed from Bristol in a small ship called the "Matthew". After thirty-five days at sea, they reached land. John was sure it was Asia. He went ashore to explore. After one month sailing up and down the coast John sailed back to Bristol with news of his discovery.

A modern picture of the "Matthew", the night before she left Bristol on her famous voyage.

Newfoundland's main harbour today

John became famous. He was called the "Grand Admiral". King Henry gave him a reward of £20 a year. People called John's land the "new found land". They believed it was part of Asia.

But the land he had really found was North America. John Cabot was the first person from England to actually set foot on the mainland of North America. He probably landed on the large island of Newfoundland, which is part of Canada.

The next year, John set out again to the "new found land", with a fleet of five ships. Only one ship came back. What happened to John Cabot and the other ships is a mystery. Nothing was ever heard of them again. Perhaps they sank in a storm. Perhaps they hit icebergs. Or perhaps they did reach land, but were unable to return. It was such a long time ago, no one will ever know what did happen.

A church window in Bristol, with pictures of John Cabot, his sons and the "Matthew".

What happened to the "Matthew"? John's little ship did not go with him on his last voyage. Instead it became a transport ship, taking goods for many years to France and Ireland.

A modern copy of the "Matthew" was built to sail to North America in 1997, exactly 500 years after John Cabot.

Important dates

In this list of dates, the letter "c" before a date means "circa". This is the Latin word for "about". For example, "c.1450" means "about 1450".

c.1450	Giovanni Caboto was born in Italy
c.1460	He went to live in Venice, Italy
1476	He became a citizen of Venice
c.1482–84	He married Mattea, a lady from Venice
1480s	His three sons were born
1480s	He sailed ships in the Mediterranean Sea
1480s	He travelled in secret to Mecca
c.1490	He went to live in Valencia, Spain
1492	Christopher Columbus sailed from Spain across the Atlantic Ocean. He landed in the West Indies, which he thought was in Asia
1493–95	Giovanni Caboto and his family moved to Bristol, in England. He changed his name to John Cabot
1496	King Henry VII and the merchants of Bristol paid for him to go on a voyage in search of Asia
1496	His first voyage ended in failure
1497	On his second voyage he reached North America in the "Matthew"
1498	He died on his third voyage
1997	A modern copy of the "Matthew" built to sail to Newfoundland, Canada

Keywords

Atlantic Ocean
the second largest ocean in the world

canal
a waterway used for transport

merchant
someone who buys and sells goods

port
a place where ships sail from

Index